73

The New Clean
a collection of poetry

❦

by Jon Sands

Write Bloody Publishing
America's Independent Press

Long Beach, CA

writebloody.com

Sands, Jon.
1ˢᵗ edition.
ISBN: 978-1-935904-26-7

Interior Layout by Lea C. Deschenes
Cover Designed by Joshua Grieve and Abe Sands
Author Photo by Jonathan Weiskopf
Proofread by Sarah Kay and Jennifer Roach
Edited by Jeanann Verlee, Adam Falkner, Roger Bonair-Agard and Derrick Brown
Type set in Helvetica by Linotype and Bergamo: www.theleagueofmoveabletype.com

Special thanks to Lightning Bolt Donor, Weston Renoud

Printed in Tennessee, USA

Write Bloody Publishing
Long Beach, CA
Support Independent Presses
writebloody.com

To contact the author, send an email to writebloody@gmail.com

For Joshua and Kathy Sands,
and the remarkable line of stories,
told and untold,
that led us to them.

THE NEW CLEAN

*"I pass death with the dying, and birth with the new-washed babe....
and am not contained between my hat and boots."*
—*Walt Whitman*

THE NEW CLEAN

WHITE BOY
after Angel Nafis after Terrance Hayes

White boy knows all the lyrics.
White boy don't know the room.
White boy working his steps.
White boys get off at 86th Street.
White boy stay on some, "Everyone *but* me, right?"
White boy incidental gentrify.
White boy coffee shop Bed-Stuy.
White boy vegan.
White boy hot sauce on everything.
White boy black music.
White boy black friends.
White boy Rosetta Stone.
White boy scared to see a documentary.
White boy your problem.
White boy with a steady hand.
White boy cuts in line 'cause he's ready to order.
White boy finally knows he's a white boy.
White boy knows all the words to the song.
White boy probably thinks the song is about him.
White boy bought an extra zip-up.
White boy holes in his boxers.
White boy holes in a lot of shit.
White boy off limits.
White boy knows every exit.
White boy 4.5 40 with two left feet.
White boy eats the last French fry.
White boy scored the CD, book, and T-shirt—presale.
White boy clean as a sunrise.
White boy too fly for guilty.
White boy too guilty for fly.

White boy all good 'til history.
White boy all good 'til Utica Avenue.
White boy safe in this Whole Foods.
White boy third base with an eye on the plate.
White boy not what you thought.
White boy bike dodging traffic.
White boy tickets to the mud fight.
Thought he was the only one
wouldn't get dirty.

TRUTH PARADE

It's a puzzle. Play with me.
— Jeanann Verlee

If my left wrist was 360 degrees of rind
pulled slowly from a grapefruit,
I would eat my bones with a sharp spoon.

If my knees were New York City,
I'd run in my sleep
and never to the doctor.

If the crook of my right elbow was a dinner party,
I would only invite crazy people. I'd soak their feet
in cherry juice and stuff them with macaroni.

If my lifeline was the Ohio River, I would wash Cincinnati
eighty-three times a day, until Buffalo Wild Wings sparkled
like a fraternity of brand-new quarters.

If my heart was an uptown 4 express train, two things:
I would never have to write this poem.
I'd only go to East 77th on the late-night.

If my poems were a song, they'd be Little Richard's.
Extra slow. A song I let simmer
on the stove for thirty-six hours.

If my penis was a city block, I'd like it to be in Brooklyn.
If the back of my eyes were the front, I still wouldn't know
where I'm going to live next year.

If my nose was the freshest strawberry in Spanish Harlem,
I'd bathe it in chocolate sweeter than the first of April.
I wouldn't let you have one bite.

ON THE BUS IN QUEENS

She tells me, *The MTA is mafia. People don't keep their receipts on them metro cards. Stupids. Then the card don't work, and whadyou got?* She's speaking my language right now. *Mah card don't work, right? I just tell the booth lady or whatever, and each time they give you this envelope, right? "We're sorry your card don't work and shit; here's the form you got to mail." But I don't mail the form, right? 'Cause they let you go through! Tricky though, right? 'Cause you got to remember who you hit already. I'm not walkin' ten blocks to the next station. In this neighborhood? Ha! So I flip the game on 'em, right? I gotta pull my hair up like this, or buy some sunglasses, or tawk layeek thees. I tell 'em "Iyeem frum Eengland eynd mayh cawrd iss browkeen. Iyee juust 'ate Ahmeareekah." And the booth lady's like, "Aww, I'm sorry you're having a bad visit." 'Cause I got my bag wit' me and shit, right? And I can't be like, "Don't feel bad booth lady. I'm just tryna get on the train." 'Cause I'm tryna get on the train, right? These cards here are just too expensive. I gotta ask my husband for money for more metros, but he don't do shit. He just smokes weed. Like, that's the only shit he do. He's Dominican. He tells me his parents are wiring him money, but then he just smokes weed! People think that's just some heroin shit. You can be addicted to weed. Like, I've never seen anyone have more reasons to smoke. He'll be like, "I gotta smoke," and I'm like, "Why?" and he's like, "'Cause you just woke me up!" "This dude just made me so mad, I gotta smoke." "That girl's wearin' jeans, I gotta smoke." "Spring Break, I gotta smoke." And he ain't even in school! It wasn't enough a while ago, he started fuckin' wit' cocaine. I said, "You can't do that in this house. Not around our beautiful daughter." Her name is Jaquelah. He's better on that shit now, and I love him. People tell me, "Why you ain't leave him when you know he ain't shit?" It ain't that they wrong, it's jus' they don't know. You can be right and not know at the same time, right? You see that dude screamin' in the front up there?* She whispers, *It's crack. He's from my old neighborhood. Always in public decreein' some shit. He needs to decree some shit on his time. Stop decreein' shit on my time. It's two o'clock, I got a place to be. My husband's twenty-five and don't do shit.*

20

I likes 'em young though, right? I'm a cougar. Or like a cougarah. Can't fuck with the old ones, smellin' like Ben-Gay and shit. Ha! I needs 'em with that stamina. You gettin' on that train? That train ride so long you get off a year older than you got on. Better have four books or some shit. No train. Not for me. Not Thursdays. I'll see you later though, baby. And I say, "Yo, you know you're a poet, right?" I think she thought I said prophet. *I know that's true! I know that.*

EXACTLY WHAT I'M THINKING

after Pablo Neruda

Why can't ceramic bowls eat fruit salad out of me?
Why can't I ever get my watch to its appointments on time?
Why can't *Braveheart* be a little embarrassed by how much
    it liked me?
Why isn't rent money concerned if I'll be ready this Saturday?

Why can't my bedroom only really be itself around me?
What if my clothes are just using me to look fresh?
Why isn't my roommate proud of me for coming home drunk
    and eating his food?
What if I shit on a bird?

What if the floor and ceiling could kiss?
What if my dreams always forget me?
What if God isn't convinced I'm real, and loses sleep over it?
What if my alarm clock could sleep in?

Why can't my six-week-old nephew just talk already?
Why can't sex say that I change everything?
Why can't love fall madly in Jon?

HIGHWAY 71

The 50-by-70 foot billboard
grazing uncut grass on the shoulder
of a South Nowhere, Ohio freeway
asks you, personally,
If you died today, where would you spend eternity?

You consider it a hypothetical question.
The way one asks,
If you could have sex with any movie star
for twenty-four straight hours,
who would you choose?

Save that a billboard asked a question
to which it already knew the answer.
Save that exactly 19.6 miles southwest
on the same grass
from the same freeway
stands a rooftop
blanketed over by what is on record
as the largest permanent display
of a confederate flag in the nation—
which is to say,
the world.

The highway clears its throat,
and as one more anonymous insect exits life
on the crusted windshield of the 1993 Camry
in which you sit passenger,
another billboard informs you,
Hell is real.

A LIST OF THINGS I LOST ON THE ROAD

White V-neck with
purple silhouette
of beautiful woman.

Grandma sunglasses.

Heart-shaped sunglasses.

Four-dollar aviator sunglasses.

(All my sunglasses: four dollars.)

Bought new sunglasses. Keep those.
Picture me rollin'.

Inside-out gray T-shirt puts
lightning bolts against my chest.

Phone call outside San Jose.
Voluntarily.

Black fleece. Passport in pocket.
Months later, passport arrives.
No fleece.

Checkbook. Got new checkbook.
Blue. Fancy. Switched accounts
before you spent my money.[1]

Green T-shirt.
Hand grenade over stomach.
Get this:

---

1   *You* most likely denotes hardwood under someone's futon in Arizona.

grenade made of mixed tapes.
Like boom!
(Zappa boom.)

Copy of *My American Kundiman*.

Green scarf knitted for Father
in 1984. (Year, not book.)

Red scarf. Not actually mine.

Canteen.
Genuine article.
From cowboy superstore in Chicago.
Beside 30-by-30-foot wall of leather gun holsters.
In Chicago for one week.
(Where are the cowboys?)

Four toothbrushes. Keep them.
If you have sunglasses,
will send picture.
Invitation to erect shrine.

Leg warmers. For her. Blue
like Caribbean Spring.
Was going to mail as gift.
Instead wrapped in paper bag,
handed to new couple on bus
from Vancouver to Seattle.

Haiku:
I almost lost my
new Hafiz socks. They match The
Gift. But I found those.

DUSK

Me: Are you there?
Her: No.
Me: Your status says you're allergic to stars.
Her: Where do you live?
Me: Ohio.
Her: Are there bushes there?
Me: Like presidents?
Her: Like bushes.
Me: As many as I have fingers, right outside my window.
Her: What color are they?
Me: All the colors the sky makes, but mostly green.
Her: Are there hearts there?
Me: I hear them shuffling at night sometimes,
    but they sound just like wind on my chimes.
Her: So you never know.
Me: So I never know.
Her: Do you have one?
Me: I do.
Her: Where does it live?
Me: I feel like I've known you before.
Her: That makes one of us.
Me: You don't have a where?
Her: I'm a traveler.
Me: Am I dreaming right now?
Her: Can you feel your arms?
Me: There are definitely two strings
    attached at my shoulders that help me love.
Her: Can you feel *them*?
Me: I must be dreaming.
Her: Do you miss me?
Me: So I have known you.

Her: Do you
     miss me?
Me: Even when I don't know I'm doing it.
Her: If you could lie right now, would you?
Me: But I can't.
Her: I need to know.
Me: But I can't.
Her: I'll be all the way gone soon. Not just mostly.
Me: That's when I'll miss you most.
Her: You can find me.
Me: That's when I'll miss you most.

EMPTY

after artist Adrian Piper

Someone just put their Diet Coke on me. Actually, they
put it on my absence. I am made of a tunnel. I am made
of a window. Today, Mr. Poet, you are made of a
turquoise sweatshirt. Today, you are made of a headache,
because last night you were made of three tequila shots.
Today, I'm made of a Diet Coke bottle. I call it my little
NutraSweetheart. I'm made of brick in here. Sometimes,
Mr. Turquoise Poet, I wish your outsides were made of
nothingness so I could see more clearly what you've
named your bricks. One is the blue your nephew keeps
in his new eyes. One, the curl your body becomes around
your second pillow on the mornings you no longer enjoy
being single. One, the night your best friends spoke the
language of karaoke and back-flipped laughter into the
walls of each bar in Ft. Greene. My promise to you
is to never stop naming. Move me outside, I'll name my
skyscrapers. Point me skyward, I'll name my planets.
Point me at yourself. Please, point me at yourself.

MY GENDER IDENTITY TIMELINE
VOLUME ONE: THE EARLY CHILDHOOD YEARS
after Tara Hardy

Chapter 1
Dad has a penis, too. His penis is much larger than my penis. His body is larger than my body. His penis would look ridiculous on my body. I don't want my body to be that big. Just my penis. Whenever Dad takes me to the restroom, it's penis o'clock.

Chapter 2
Mom has a vagina I don't have. Mom says she saw her mom's vagina *so much* when Mom was my age. Mom watches TV with her vagina. She cooks with her vagina, too, sometimes. Mom's vagina taught me vaginas are gigantic mounds of hair. Sometimes you can still see Mom's vagina when she wears a bathing suit. Mom wants me to be comfortable around her vagina. She doesn't want us to shake hands, but she wants us to be friends.

Chapter 3
I don't know what sex is, but I'm beginning to suspect who's involved. Penises seem to be everywhere these days. All my brothers have one. There are five of us. Each penis looks like the toes on dad's foot, in ascending order. I don't have two sisters, or even one. People always apologize to Mom. They laugh while they apologize. Mostly it's bank tellers and waitresses. I wonder if mom's vagina ever gets lonely.

Chapter 4
I slept at Bobby's house tonight. It's the first time I've seen midnight in Cincinnati from someone else's bed. Penis was the game of the night. More fun than Ghost in the Graveyard; we laughed for four straight hours. We held each other's penises like they were secrets. Or marbles. Or secret marbles.

Chapter 5

I had a dream about Elise last night. She walked up the stairs while I was asleep, and instead of saying hello, or asking about my lunchbox, she was naked, and lay down flat on my body. Then we hugged forever. I believe this is sex, but I have yet to confirm that with any authority figure. I saw Elise again in the back seat of my mom's car on the way to school. I asked her if we could do what we did in my dream. She pretended not to remember. I played along and told her the story we had written. She made the same face she makes when, by accident, someone spreads mayonnaise on her wheat bread. I'm beginning to question if hugging forever is even possible.

Chapter 6

My brother Ben wears his Speedo long after swim practice is over. The rest of us have trunks that stop at our knees. We also care about the Cincinnati Bengals. Ben only pretends to care when he feels lonely. But we share a bedroom, a closet, and a sense of adventure. All of his friends are girls, who also know nothing about the Cincinnati Bengals. Our elementary school held a talent show. Ben performed "Big Girls Don't Cry" to a sold-out auditorium.

Chapter 7

This afternoon, my brother Abe played me a VHS tape. Two women were in a garden talking about plants. They were naked so fast. I reached for more Chex Mix without being hungry. A man saw them through a fence. Then his penis was *everywhere*. The label on the tape said "M★A★S★H Episodes." I asked Mrs. Connell what it means when the whole world keeps a secret. She said, *We call that a conspiracy.*

Chapter 8

Ben and I do not like each other tonight. It began when I changed the channel on our radio, and refused to turn it back. We were supposed to be asleep. I said, *I hate sharing this room with you.* He said, *I hate that you were born.* I said, *I hate you.* We lay in our beds, silent for long enough to realize we could no longer see our own hands. He called me *fat*. I called him a *faggot*. Then it was over.

*"After you make the love you dream of making
You come home to clean your closets
And make sure to keep the phone nearby
Just in case you bump into half of something
That will bring you back and
Hit you where it hurts"*

—Willie Perdomo

EPITHALAMION:
FOR MOLLIE AND MY BROTHER JACOB

February 28, 2009

Years after my grandmother Grace had left us, my
grandfather remained, carrying Alzheimer's in one of
his many suitcases. In the hours when dream and reality
were not cooperating, those nearest the care-giving
would say, *Grandpa! Grandpa! What's the best thing
you ever did?* He would pause—his body now a more
contorted exclamation point—and reply, *Marrying Grace.*

Or

when the disease would not allow him her absence, the
gentle in his eyes would find that of the requester—now
playing the role of b*eautiful woman* to whom he had been
joined for fifty-six years, twelve children, one World War—
he would reply, *Marrying you.*

Love will shave less important details like facts or
presence. It will be young. It will lay you flat on the grass,
staring up at a jet-black *out-there*, into meringue dance
floors where fingers swallow hips, your head nearly
skims the floor when he dips you, and your legs dance
together so positive you have to call it *love* or *religion*.
It will place you on sidewalks that lead toward *away*,
a wake of regret smudged across the surrounding
pavement. Your mouth will say, *I'm sorry.* Your hands,
I was wrong. Eyes, *I love you after everything.* Your
eyes will mean laugh, and laugh will mean forgive.
It will find you at two a.m. in Wisconsin, when neither
of you lives in Wisconsin, kneeling beside a couch. She
is almost asleep now. There is a plastic gold ring in

your palm. You are whispering, *I want to spend the rest of my life with you.* Or sometimes the couch becomes Nebraska. The floor becomes Houston. The ring is not plastic, or even tangible. It is just the distance of a protracted line waiting to be rolled into a circle. But it still *is*. And love still is a roller coaster, the giant wooden roller coaster at King's Island, even though you don't ride roller coasters, but she loves them, and she laughs, which makes you laugh, every time.

The stories and the characters, the characters and the details, will smooth through your fingers like a child in a sandbox—somewhere, your grandchildren will find you. They will ask you what sits at the top of the right decisions you plucked from all the wrong ones; a trace of gentle in your eyes, you will reply:

Marrying Mollie.
Marrying Jacob.

Or, depending on the day,
Marrying you.

APRIL 23RD

I sit outside a New York City sandwich
shop. There is a crisp, sun-filled bench.
This is where I am seated. Beside me,

a dog tied to that bench.
This is not my dog. But he is cute,
all circle-eye and wag-tail.

He is staring at me. There is a thin, open
book in my palms. It is shiny
like the metaphors that line its pages.

 I am not actually reading this book.
 Eighth Avenue is far too busy to make out the words.

She most certainly believes this to be my dog.
She does not know I am not reading this shiny book.
None of this holds any bearing.

Her smile rings through my ears like beat-box,
making pickup lines of all these factors
I cannot control.

We are both smiling. Our prayers,
a gift tucked into the city's skyline.
And such is April—

 the month we relearn to watch each other.

When it thumps through our bodies
that we have not seen another person's shoulder
while simultaneously being outside

 in over 150 days.

PARTY & BULLSHIT
after The Notorious B.I.G.

When the buttons on your shirt become smooth bullets
through each opening.

The bathroom mirror, a soothsayer specializing
in the murder of living room dance floors.

Each sidewalk from here to Atlantic-Pacific
Billy Jeans at your feet.

Every door you open tonight is a sacrifice
to gods you will never learn.

Just like you never learned *Pop* or *Lock*—
yet here you are, praying to both of them,

praising the way music does not cause amnesia,
just short-term memory loss,

and *you* too drunk for no-health-insurance.
Her hair smells too good for the bedbugs.

Your arms and the edges of your mouth know one direction, sky,
and no one holds your sunglasses against you.

You have the right to remain sexy.
To name a new dance move after everything you do:
        The Refrigerator-Open.
        The Subway-Hand-Rail.
        The Bathroom-Line.
        The Creepy-Back-Massage.

To morph this body into an exclamation point.
Alchemistical is your new vernacular—

you turn oxygen to gold.
   Shoelaces gold.
   Doorknobs gold.
   Urinal cakes...gold!

Your throat is an escalator
transferring fun both ways.

Dirty is the new clean, and this
is the cleanest apartment in Brooklyn.

ODE TO SLEEP

Last night I was drunk. Now I'm hungover. I'm going to
blame the insufficient time I spent with you. Which is more
than with anyone. Remember when you made me believe
I was trapped in a forest made of Styrofoam, then flying
(kind of like a ripped paper airplane), then getting a blowjob
from Cate Blanchett, even though she looked exactly like this
girl I went to high school with, but we both still knew she
was Cate Blanchett? Who else does that? I spend a half-hour
untying myself from you each morning. I think you know me
best. The way my body crooks into itself when I'm lonely.
You unraveling yarn ball. You slow dance magician who never
calls before you come. (On the floor of JC Penney. A two a.m.
uptown 6 train into the Bronx, eleven stops past my apartment
in East Harlem. After paying thirteen dollars to see *WALL-E*
in the movie theater.) Even writing this, hungover on an airplane,
I feel your long fingers curling over my shoulder. I wonder
where you go when I am forgetting you most. You are so
large, it must be me who does the traveling. But I return
to be lost in you—a planet of ocean, and I am a buoy
that can't stop trying to sink.

NEW YORK TRANSIT

dollarcab airtrain ratskate tunnelluge
roofskip backstroke crosswalk strollpark
bridgejump gymstep pigeondrift bikepeg
bankerback bulletride horsetrot interweb
lifeline prayerstampede skydream recorddeal
carsteal fencehop moonwalk jumpshot
papervan windowwish wirewalk rikersbus
fastbreak trashsled bootytrail whitesneaks
penthouse metrohustle firefly churchscream

"GRAB A SNACK. ENJOY THE SPACE, BUT IF YOU'RE NOT SUPPORTING US, TIME TO SPLIT."

after the sign and barista at Yippie Café, Bleecker Street, New York City

I couldn't loan you a pen if I wanted, which I don't.
I wouldn't splash if you were on fire, which
I wish you were. It's not that war, you know?
It's just peace, love, and passive aggressive.
Peace, love, and fifteen years ago.
Peace, love, and everyone got a job
but me. Buy this peace button before my eyes
stick an elbow in that temple. You don't know
what it is to have time look like tail lights on a pick-up
when you're just standing there in Albuquerque.
Love has been a four-letter word.

I don't mean to take this out on you, but
I actually do. This is the only shit that makes
the corner of my lips climb. The crease
in your khakis put a thumbtack in my heart. That fedora
has my whole face in granite mode. I'm not loaning you a pen.
The other workers stole the pens.
You know who works here? Bums.
You know who hates 'em? Me. You don't
know the wars I fought. The shit people left
on my front walk. No broom. No bleach. No
fucking road map! You need to buy a muffin
before my pocketknife buys a kidney. You need never
loiter in this store I own. My hate is fresh out the box.
Refilled more than the ice bin 'round these parts.
You wouldn't know a goddamn thing about yesterday.
You and your umbilical cord. You're just gonna' sit there

and write about me? Gonna get specific on that notepad
not three feet from my cash register? Where I work?
Which smells like dirty sock every day?
I'd tell you to get quiet for the banjo and bongo on stage
but I hate that shit too. Banjos and fabricated customers
are a renewable resource 'round here. Believe I got a Great Lake
of attitude out back. I dare you to love me.
I axed *that* branch from my tree decades ago.
Sixty strong. This has always been what it is.
Take this iced coffee with extra stink, and don't even think
about turning around to watch me die.

POSSIBLE

She is 27 years younger than you. Which makes you 46.
You question her about something she won't know,
like how to die gracefully, or something easier:

What does ameliorate mean? You are sure not to question her
about things she knows completely, like which cashier
at BP is least likely to ID, or what it means to be invincible,

or your own daughter's favorite late-night/blackout food,
which is to say—*her friend Elizabeth's favorite.*
Least of all do you question what she has learned.

To be 19 is to know more than you've learned, and
in this particular kitchen, that is a good thing. What you know
for certain: you live in a house with four women,

all of whom currently have their eyes closed, and it would be
difficult to imagine them knowing what you are about to know.
You've shared a bedroom with one for the better part

of three decades. The skin between her eyes and the top
of her cheekbones looks more tangled than what used to
remind you of silk. Time is time. Still, you think it unfair.

You know the neck of a nineteen-year-old is the texture of a wave
after crashing. Smoothing the sand. Sometimes a giggle
is a red light. Or punctuation at the end of a sentence.

This giggle is a water fountain, a sign that says, *You
are so thirsty.* A body is not concerned with who's to blame.
Sex with this child is not unlike swallowing your family tree

as you shimmy along the branches. A particular brand
of irreversible. You remove your loafers. Fill one more Shiraz
to the glass's lip. The call is already in the air. You could not

have known it possible your body would answer.

MY FRIEND

My Friend Lost His Fucking Cell Phone!
is going to be the title of my next movie. John Cusack
will star: phoneless, frantic, and adorable

with monologues that stretch like giant rubber bands.
White men in their twenties will say, *You know,*
I really identify with that. This IS what sadness feels like.

I don't make movies. I am a white man in my twenties.
My friend did lose his fucking cell phone.
He feels contactless, naked, deserted.

He is literally wearing no clothes in the middle
of the Atlanta airport. He's embarrassed
and seated next to his loneliness.

It feels like other travelers can see his loneliness
more than they can see him. He didn't actually
lose his fucking cell phone. He left it

in the backseat of an Acura in North Carolina.
They found it. They're mailing it.
But not until tomorrow. He could read emails from it.

He stuffed each person he loves into it.
He knows they're not actually inside,
but that's where he keeps them. It feels like everyone

is flying away from Atlanta except him and his loneliness.
He screamed *fuck!* so loudly the whole gate looked at him
and away from him at the same time.

Do you see what I'm getting at? I'm embarrassed.
I left my cell phone in North Carolina
and have forgotten how to feel loved without it.

I can't believe something that doesn't matter
matters this much. It's never about what it's about. But why
did I imagine breaking the door off the bathroom stall

with my suitcase? Why am I about to cry in a city
where I don't know anyone? Why aren't my own hands enough?
How did my body change this much since morning?

ELEGY

for Marge and Nathan Sands

I order potatoes and bacon across from you and Grandpa
on West 23rd Street—I still eat bacon, and don't yet live
in this city that is an ocean which drops welcome home
letters on E trains from JFK, reading, *I didn't know you
were gone. I don't know you're back.*

Today, I am eleven. Grandma, you live here. Your toast
*isn't quite golden brown. They said it would be five minutes on
the corned beef hash. It was eight. The cash register is ringing
too loud, and what is this music anyway!?* They know your
absurdly purple, gigantic prescription sunglasses by name,
have your table ready. I trust each busboy and host, and
will take my time to learn smiling can be a job description.

You live in an apartment I don't, and can't know one day
I will. I'll live there so hard, I'll order a fifty sack and
smoke out the delivery boy in the living room. So hard,
when I go on a first date with Crazy Lucy from Detroit
and we fight the whole night like you and Grandpa, then
she rocks the worst blowjob I don't even want, asks if she
should leave, even though it's 5:35 in the morning now,
I'll say she can stay—because it's my apartment. When she
starts snoring like she's trying to wake my brother and his
boyfriend in the next room, I'll take my pillow and sleep
on my couch—because by then it will be my couch.

But, today, even from New York, my home in Cincinnati
is still folding around me like an egg. It isn't yet the city
in which my father will leave my mother. Or the city to
which he'll return. Or the two weeks between that I won't
remember. Or the two weeks after he comes home but

isn't really home. Or the decade we'll spend pretending it
didn't happen. Or the years I will immediately fall asleep
each time my mother mentions her own sadness.

Grandma, this is the year Heather has her aneurism:
they'll say she was brain dead in the ambulance, flatlined
by the hospital. A week before, I'll imagine dipping my
chubby fingers into the blue pools of her eyes just to feel
how they're possible, dream of her strawberry curls with
unending wonderment, convinced she might let me move
into them. I'll wish her funeral were open casket. They'll
play *One Sweet Day*, and I'll know Boys II Men wrote this
for me.

Today though, it's you, me, and Grandpa headed uptown
to the museums. You love each other, because why else
would you still be here? You'll scream at him to *give
the horn!* to the whole West Side. He'll be driving an '89
Toyota Camry I don't know will be mine by high school,
when it has rusted doors and stalls each time I turn left at
an intersection with oncoming traffic—Grandpa is *going
too slow!* And *Nat, the light is red! Nat, the light is green!* And
who but you has permission to screech his name like an
irascible mantra? And he does make you laugh, sometimes
by not saying anything.

When he falls into the population of those holding keys
to the big question, years from now, *now*—where even
when he's not thinking, he looks like he's thinking. When
he's not detached, he looks detached. When he's not
mourning a life that never quite paid his due promise.
When he does pass, and I accompany you on a flight back
to a nursing home in Cincinnati, a city that by then will
call to me like a slow dying, you'll say, *It's been seventy years.
I don't know who I am without Nat.*

I'll tell you, *History doesn't remember us that way. We'll*
remember how you swirled out of this world together.
We will remember you together—thus you are.
Before falling asleep against the window, you'll say, *Jon,*
that sounds very poetic. But it still doesn't help.

It still doesn't help.

*Horizon's blue, and
shit. But I fall in love with
my own prints in snow.*

WHAT I KNOW

Don't push me, 'cause I'm close to the edge.
— Grandmaster Flash

Feels like dawn, but it's 3:45 on my watch.
Priority was to have an extra-fly watch.

Nobody's got more hours than yesterday's got—
see my body become less alive on my watch.

My granddad paid rent—first day each month in this house.
Came home from Europe. Said, *Those men died on my watch.*

Read news. Coffee black. Silence zipped like a raincoat.
My dad next to his brother never tried to cry, *Watch.*

Held *my* brother tight when I left Boston last month.
Said, *I love you, dude.* But kept an eye on my watch.

Said, *I understand no one makes it out alive.*
I swore on lost time, but I lied on my watch.

I drank my loving cup. I don't return phone calls,
but make certain my shoes match my tie and my watch.

Throw game as if I'm the one kid not getting old.
Think my ankles won't break when they ride the sky, watch.

This unnamed siren song. Bullet I can't dance through.
Bags'll droop under my eyes like they're tied to my watch.

It comes naked as your own skin. Just love. Just love.
You just have the people you've loved when you die, watch.

PIADINA, TENTH STREET, NEW YORK CITY
for Ox

Some nights the $50 in your jeans doesn't wish to leave in increments. You've had pockets for Mamoun's (on St. Marks where you can get $2.50 pita stuffed like a catcher's mitt), discount Sierra Nevada, and $2 tip on the one you get free ('cause this is your spot).

You're with a man who is close as the blood through your arteries. Has been since eighth grade, when y'all dared him to get butt-naked and ask your older brother (and a kitchen of friends) if they had any *Juicy Juice*. You, he, and Warner used to trade turns in the small room of the basement with your other brother's porno. One time you and Warner banged the window (hidden behind the bushes in the front yard) just to see how fast he could race into his clothes if you caught him doing something he already knew you knew.

He'd pin older boys against a drinking fountain for talking to you without smiling. You got a ten-day suspension at Winter Formal, partly for delivering a ninth-grader (who supposedly called his little brother a kike at the football game) into the brick skin of the bathroom wall (but mostly for the nine shots of 151). New Years was always the night your whole crew was right enough to say, *I love you.*

Bread that tumbles oven to olive oil (laced with crushed red pepper). White wine-red wine, an antipasti you can't pronounce so you name it your *Little Italian Quesadilla*— whisper into the crust of its ear, *I'ma eat you. Don't even worry about that.* Some nights you are paying to pretend this is how you always eat. When you taste the marinara your gnocchi is backstroking through, you know why you're both here. It is so clear this is the only life you are currently living, and without him it wouldn't be yours.

The ingredient nestled like a comforter against the back of your mouth is time. The tomato and basil settled against the stovetop like a rocking chair to the tune of nine hours—each minute, a melting together of the plump red stories you now taste. Fashioning what was once delicious into inexplicable magic. It's the one item on that gourmet list they didn't buy.

I LEARN WHAT A BATSMAN IS
JUST AS THE MUSHROOMS KICK IN

I wasn't certain, but now I'm positive:
the mushrooms *have* kicked in.
I've never witnessed a cricket match,
so I'm not sure what is happening
among these nineteen Indian men in Ft. Greene Park
scrambling each way across a large oval of dirt,
I imagine at some point had grass. Ed's head
is using the space between my shoulder blades
as a pillow. Behind the game is a single tree
whose name I imagine to be Cesar, partly
because I am speaking to him. He says
he is 150 years older than I am.
He used to be sad his friends all had roots
and not feet or motors. He says, *Jon, Jon, Jon.*
Imagine if every person you loved woke in their beds
each morning, then stayed there until it was time
to sleep again—all the while, slowly getting larger.
Now imagine you have no friends because they are all
lying in these beds. Imagine never touching
your mother's forearm. The knots in the bark I imagine
to be eyes hint at a glossiness. *Not all trees can rise*
in the forest, he whispers. And I wonder if trees like Cesar
have special names for the ones in the forest,
the way we have celebrities. The cricket ball smacks
him in the stomach. He doesn't seem to mind anymore.
He's grown to appreciate tiny things against his skin—
a seething gang of fire ants, the small of a back reading
in the afternoon, the random boy on mushrooms—
makes him feel less alone. There is a man now
behind Cesar who has spilled all the contents

of his Styrofoam cooler onto the concrete
walkway, making a tiny ocean of beer,
meat, and vegetables. We stop talking
as Ed's face sprouts from my back. *Yo,
if we help that dude, can we have some of his shit?*
The audience roars with laughter.
Ed is their favorite character.

I WIN
for Danny Sherrard

My friend Danny puts hot sauce on cereal.
So I spread a dollop across my morning
grapefruit. If there were two faucets
in his kitchen and one gushed
green chili paste,
that would be just fine.
At restaurants, I get extra
Habañero Fireball. Danny sends
the waiter for *Dave's Insanity
Sauce*—we'll order two or three more
bottles as if they're on the wine list.
Long ago, told the taste receptors
on our tongues they were on their own.
Even his footsteps seem to have been
sprinkled with crushed red pepper.
We pour spicy mountain ranges onto sandwiches
as if some sort of reward awaits.
Currently, I'm in the bathroom, but I brushed
the waiter as he was moving
toward our corner table. I said,
I'll take the drunken noodles.
Oh, and make mine as spicy as his.

I put my hand on the waiter's shoulder.
And then a little spicier.

WE DON'T MAKE THE SKY, SIR

We make giant pieces of metal that enter the sky.
I'm not Mother Nature. If there's snow in Cincinnati,
can't touch down. Snow today? No plane. Tomorrow?
The same. We don't own the sky, God does. God and
TSA. Look at the name on this ticket anyways: Jon.
I can say what won't fly: Jonathan, unless five letters
escape from his birth certificate. Now lean in and let me
tell you something real good so you hear it. I know
the word "fuck" in fifty-seven different languages.
I am not judge, don't legislate business, half the time
don't even agree, but there is such a thing as order,
and ten years back—folks took it on their own to put two
flying metal slabs into two buildings, and there were
bird owners in those buildings. Shoe salesmen, people
who had never eaten crème brulee, who were allergic to
cherries, cut the crust off liverwurst sandwiches and put
children named Luke, Shameekah, or Becca onto shiny
yellow busses each morning, so I need you to plug your
eyeballs into that ferris wheel and roll them back to this
desk here. This world is not for people who always
want to *choose* which foot goes forward, and to where.
You know how many feet are out there? Think of only
the feet you know. You trust where they drag all those
bodies? No snow, no go, those are facts. You made it
political, sir. And I'm saying, someone's gonna do it.
Drop the big one from Delta, Jet Blue, or Air France,
and I'll tell you whose eyes they *won't* have looked into.
So when we say *spread 'em*, you better already know
how wide. You don't want to be the ruler, just the
exception, the one always asking to speak to a supervisor.
I am the supervisor, and she'd tell you the same thing.

Take a number, sir. Take a deep breath, *sir*, take every single thing out of your fucking pockets. This isn't about snow, and it certainly isn't about you.

PASSOVER (OR THURSDAY)

I ate a burrito for dinner tonight.
My family rearranged the entire
Jewish calendar for Passover
to fall on a weekend.
It was more convenient for us.

We treat our Jewish like a distant cousin
we invite to weddings and reunions,
where it sits at a corner table,
finishes the potatoes while the rest of us
electric slide into another cocktail.

I never thought to count, but if I had,
I imagine I could say *I have gone 94 days
without my Judaism being a factor.*
Moses carried the Israelites
through the Egyptian desert for 40 years.

When I recite from a Haggadah, the part
that gets me is: children of Israel
have read this document for more
than two millennium. I am a Gemini. I am a
Vegetarian. I am a Poet. I am Jewish.

I have procured so many definitions,
it's a wonder I fit in my apartment. I once asked
a Gentile who had been my girlfriend for seven months
(over a Caesar salad) if she believed Jesus Christ
died for her sins. I don't remember

if it was Sunday. But if it was, we had spent
the entire morning wrapped around each others' limbs
like rope. Ultimately, she said yes. Then we went
to the movies, or a park bench, or we didn't go
anywhere. We never thought to discuss it again.

THE SHOW

for Adam Falkner

We cannot forgive them—
these
sixth-grade intruders of our handball game.
It is *our* court.

These
short-legged, loudmouth comedians—not one understands
it is our court.
Can't see Adam swing game-point ready despite

short-legged, loudmouth comedians—not one understands
how *beautiful* it is that grown folk play handball.
Can't see Adam swing, game-point ready despite
nine-to-fives and late-night Pacifico.

(How beautiful it is that grown folk play handball.)
We move, dive, laugh like sixth graders immune to
nine-to-fives and late-night Pacifico.
We are bull riders trying to outlast our bucking youth.

They move, dive, laugh like sixth graders immune to
our quest and our icy stares.
We are bull riders trying to outlast our bucking youth.
They slice through our game like they own

our quest and our icy stares.
They are sheriff of the city we no longer run.
They slice through our game like they own
the dust in our footprints. We know

they sheriff this city. We no longer run
the show.

They are the dust in our footprints—we know,
we used to be them.

The Show:
Sixth-grade intruders of our handball game.
We used to be them.
We cannot forgive them.

TURBULENCE

As the wheels release the concrete, I remember,
not so much to make peace with life, but to accept
death. To accept what comes. My grandfather was
my age in 1945, a corporal in Germany. At his charge:
a handful of ammunition soldiers, four munitions trucks,
over six hundred hidden wishes to arrive home
with a beating heart, and limbs enough to envelope
another's entire body.

The story goes: February 17, 3:46 in the afternoon.
No one saw the bomb gently slide from the truck,
soon to detonate, to firmly cork the gap between
a soldier's nightmare and a soldier's reality. Or at
the very least—no one saw it soon enough.
Twenty-five men would never again see their
elbows, toenails, thighs. Twenty-five more would
never see anything. Ever again. Corporal Nathan
Leonard Sands, however, stood in the shower,
softly humming an old Bing Crosby tune, which at
the time was not so old. Still quite unaware of the
fact that this would be a very long day.

I was always told, *When it is your time to go—that
is your time.* Do not weep at your fate. Do not negotiate
with random deities. Tighten your belt and receive.
It will undoubtedly receive you back. It happens to
the best of us. There is an expected ding of the fasten-
seatbelt sign. Each thirty-foot drop of this airliner has
a new name.

Drop: Sex, in an exquisite place: the top of the Eiffel Tower.
Drop: The delicate hand attached to a tiny person that I made.

Drop: Love. The real thing. The kind that makes you stay
  when every limb claws for the door.
Drop: Wrinkled stories of distant war, Cincinnati bedside.
  A man in his twilight.

The businessman to my side: drilled into his armrest.
The thin redhead to my back: leafing through a magazine
with her eyes closed. The thirteen-month-old to my front:
screaming like she's trying to save something. And me:
the scared, stubborn boy who never learns his lessons.
I tighten the wrinkles around my eyes, pray to whatever
god will have me.

THE DAY TIME LEFT

Pumpernickel
　　alarm on
　　　　baker's oven
　　　　　　never dings.
　　　　　　Kitchen smells
　　　　delicious
　　always.
Six-year-old
breath-holder
　　in Jefferson
　　　　Pool lives
　　　　　　underwater.
　　　　　　B-boy
　　　　swirling
　　concrete at
Coney Island:
his head is
　　new feet.
　　　　Man injecting
　　　　　　in Starbucks
　　　　　　bathroom
　　　　doesn't
　　float down.
Husband
checked into
　　Chelsea
　　　　Hotel with
　　　　　　not-wife
　　　　　　has new
　　　　forever.
　　North Pole

glacier
keeps ice.
    Entire L
        train is
            mole people.
            Fourth date
          Ft. Greene Park
    lucky to be
in love.
Woman off
    Triborough
        Bridge
            becomes dove.
            Seventy-three-
          year-old fingers
    interlocked
in turbulence
seven miles
    over Atlantic
        Ocean. The jet
          plane nestled
          atop cloud like
       a penny in
    God's loafer.

"I'll make a new world here so that I never have to go home again!"
— Harper, Angels in America

AM

I am rye, laced into the first bottle of whiskey. Do not touch me with kid gloves. I am opaque black ink on the first quill transcribing The Bible like I was possessed by God. I am possessed by God. Brother, I am your moment. The most magnificent butterfly of a basketball player ever to lace sneakers. With the flu. On the brink of fainting. Still dropping thirty-eight on a befuddled Utah so my thumb would not go ringless. I am Muhammad Ali not given that chance for the three best years of my life. Not fighting in a war because my war was in Louisville, Kentucky. My war was in Birmingham, Alabama—and it was not over; the smooth scratch of Etta James' high notes screaming, *You won't catch me, but you will never finish running*; the straw on Nat Turner's back; any moment that drills your sternum like a rusted chisel promising, *Anything is better than this.*

I am my older brother—a sophomore in high school, seating his sibling, whispering, *This is what I am, and I love myself.* His eyes when I still used *faggot* as slang for the last time in my life. I am old-tattered-trenchcoat on a woman wearing her story on the 6 train. The dragon, fire-breathing-defiance, Noah turned away from his ark because I don't take no shit; two eleven-year-olds on the J/M/Z breakdancing for their lives over the Williamsburg Bridge. Do not tell me I have not been here—I *am* been here. I am New Jersey transit, a fifth of Jim Beam, and a raspy paper bag. I am the stapled mouth of my little cousin—and each teenager who steals themselves from a universe that has not taught them how to scream. I am faceless bullets fired from crooked guns in the name of everything human, iceberg lettuce spooning the 1996 bun of the first Big Mac served in India, the last star on Orion's belt making me see my mother's eyes when she smiles so hard it looks like she's crying. I am the view of any sunset, on any skyline, from any highway, which still spells *Cincinnati* in cursive across my eyeballs.

Pretend for one moment you are me, because you are. I have always been your moment. The first time. Anytime this universe exploded inside your stomach and you could not stop saying, *love, love,* and *love,* and *you.*

A WORKING LIST OF THINGS
I WILL NEVER TELL YOU

When I said I wasn't with another woman
the January after we fell in love for the third time,
it's because it wasn't actual sex.

In the February that began our radio silence,
it was actual sex. I hate the tight shirts
that go below your waistline.

Not only do they make you look too young,
but then your torso is a giraffe's neck attached to tiny legs.
I screamed at myself in the subway

for writing poems about you still.
I made a scene. I think about you almost
each morning, and roughly every five days,

I still believe you're there.
I still masturbate to you.
When we got really bad,

I would put another coat of mop water on the floor of the bar
to make sure you were asleep when I got to my side of the bed.
You are the only person to whom I've lied, knowing

I was telling the truth. I miss the way your neck
wraps around my face like a cave we are both lost in.
I remember when you said being with me

is like being alone with company.
My friend Sarah wrote a poem about pink ponies.
I'm scared you're my pink pony.

Hers is dead. It is really sad. You're not dead.
You live in Ohio, or Washington, or wherever.
You are a shadow my body leaves on other girls.

I have a growing queue of things I know
will make you laugh and I don't know where to put them.
I mourn like you're dead. If you had asked me to stay,

I would not have said *No*.
It would never mean *Yes*.

THE FISHERMEN
for JV CH AF EH EM

Sometimes you dance slow with your best friend
while a woman you love differently than you love Etta James
sings *At Last* into a karaoke machine
like she wrote it in the bathroom.
Sometimes every person you know is drunk enough;
it becomes a new definition for sober.

There is a bar on the west side of Brooklyn
the fishermen call home (or they used to,
when Brooklyn had fishermen), a lighthouse carrying them back
to their whiskey. Sometimes, there is tonight.
We are six people who make footsteps that never disappear.
Can you imagine the lines we have drawn to get here?

There are people who have called us their homes.
Tonight, there is family in the oxygen. Sometimes,
two people *is* its own person. It has a lifespan,
it gets hungry, it too, can lie underneath its sheets
and wonder how it can still feel alone—
sometimes it is more.

There is a phone booth in the bar that seats one.
Six of us scramble inside, crawl up the walls
until even our drinks fit, our bodies rediscovering
what it is to be possible. It is one night
when the clocks in Brooklyn begin to spill backwards,
then stop. The bartender—still as a stalagmite,

while the perfect pour stays perfect.
The couple at the corner table,
together like popsicle sticks in a freezer—

the *ovvvv* from *I love you* suspended
in the air like a vibrating chandelier.
We, with our songs, our slow dances,

our smiles—which on any other day
rotate like the swing on a jump rope—
we are the last to go, we are the last to go,

we are last—

THE MIRROR MAYOR OF BACK-TALK CITY

Have you seen John Murillo? Dude makes me want to play
basketball in his poems. Makes me want to fly through his poems.
Like drop-step, step-slam, dunk! Michael Jordan could fly, you
know. He put 38 on the Jazz with a fever, you know. And no one
could stop that, so we put him in a Michael Jackson video. So for
once, let's not say talent. If you want to be the baddest, there's
always someone else willing to shoot free throws 'til five in the
morning—to turn concrete to NBA Finals. It's the best of 143.
They won't stop until they game-winner all of it. I'm telling you
right now, pumpkin (this is Jon speaking), if you thought there
was any other way than yours, you bought a round-trip to
misinformation. I'd like to welcome you home. I knitted you a
sweater. It's actually a sweat suit. It's actually a suit-suit. Or just a
vest. It's your chest. I'm sayin'. Can't you see I'm trying to stop?
But this feels, like, really good. Like if God thumbtacked me to
the crown of a mountain and said, *Say one thing*, this is it right
here. I'd scream the box out my voice. The gus out your esopha.
I'd lie to you just to tell you the truth. Michael Jordan had 104-
degree flu and still made John Stockton look like your uncle in the
backyard on a nine-foot hoop with a small ball. Exit sign's right
over there. It looks like a grenade. And that pin in your hand,
that's the actual pin. I'm too loose now. My arms are straight out
like a poet who sounds like a different poet. I'll send you and call
you back in the same line. I'll ban smoke in your poems then
invite Michael Jordan, and he'll show. You won't have anyone
to blame but the mirror. Don't bother looking for me. The sign on
this door says, *Disturb*. It says, *Amaze*. It says, *Be amazing*. My
whole body's inside akimbo. Ready to make mistakes. To stay.
I made you spaghetti. Pretty sure we're the sauce. So, it's just
me and you, baby. It's just me and you.

YO! (I NEED A BEAT)

after Michael Cirelli

Yo Angel! Twenty minutes late is still ten minutes early.
Yo Adam, I'ma tie Paris to the end of a balloon
    and save us a plane ticket.
Yo East Village, why I got to be so pretty just to be ugly?
Yo Cincinnati, I love you more than I actually love you.
Yo sky, I want to stab gravity.
Yo Yo,
      Yo.
Yo Cirelli, why you make me do this shit just by doin' this shit,
    as a result of other people doin' this shit?
Yo fuck, why won't you let me give you?
Yo Jeanann Verlee!
      Why your poems turn me into sparrows and clouds and shit?
Yo Thomas Fucaloro, why'd I blurb your book
    and wake up in rehab?
Yo rehab,
      why'd I blurb your book and wake up in Thomas Fucaloro?
Yo William Blake, that shit's played now.
Yo dollars, can I talk to you for a minute?
Yo January, can I live?
      And Brooklyn, why can't I get you via spaceship?
Yo anxiety, you look the same as being a dick.
Yo Grandma, we'll Charleston on the gravestone.
      Grab eye shadow.
Yo love, write me a good check.
      Yo stop sign, nuh-uh.
Yo nighttime, why so right?
Yo sleep, you owe me like five hours.
Yo terrorism, talk it out.
Yo Berenstein Brother Bear, stop telling people we're related.

Yo haters,
              boo.
Yo sunrise, never
          on the bad nights.
Yo discipline, pssshhh.
Yo drama…
we're actually using that seat.

I GOT A LETTER FROM MIDTOWN

for Jon Sands

Never been below 14th Street.
Heard you're edgy.
Heard tales of young men
with mustaches and tight pants.
Heard you draw clouds
that look like Toni Morrison.
Scribble poems about Nina Simone.
Harmonize love songs
to *your* definition of Jesus.
That you dance like grasshoppers
(or any animal with rhythm).
    Heard *art*.
    Heard *quarter notes*.
Heard you think I'm jealous.
Heard you sunrise on a Bushwick flat
after thirteen cups of Jameson.
That you walk home the whole way,
57 blocks, while the rainwater
saturates your thick blue jeans
just so you can tell the story tomorrow.
Heard you never trust a man in uniform
or any suit that isn't corduroy.
Heard they stared
at your tattooed arms on the J train.
That you were happier than you let on.
    Heard *poem*.
    Heard *step*.
    Heard *two jobs*.
    Heard *busboy*.

Paralegal.
Vegan-bookstore-cashier.
Heard Mom and Dad stopped sending checks.
Heard you moved back to South Carolina.
    To Austin.
    Back to Cincinnati.
No.
Heard you stayed put.
Carved *Lower-East-Side* into your upper thigh.
Shook yourself vulnerable.
Heard that was enough.
Heard it wasn't.
Heard you think I won't find you there.
Heard you fight me to bloody knuckle.
I've never felt the sting.
Your shine never dimmed my bright lights.
You wear me on your sneakers—
who do you think stitched the patch of your swoosh?
I am a whisper in the front pocket of your faded jeans.
Heard pretentious-adorable poet
thinks you rule the world.
Heard you know I do.
I dare you to follow through.
Have fun with your revolution.
Let me know how it turns out.
I will be arms-outstretched at your finish line.
Look around your continents. Just see
if you can stop me.

THE MONSTER I'M HIDING
UNDER MY BED SAYS

New York City has gone the way of the blues.
She says I can go to Duane Reade anytime I want.
Says feet were made facing forward for good reason.
You already know *this* world is real. You want to go
to the 1970s? Kill yourself. See if that'll do it.

WHEN I RETURN AS A GARBAGE CAN

I will make myself a comfortable bullseye
for everything dirty, constructing
tiny body parts of the unwanted:

apple core heart,
saran wrap liver,
rotten strawberry toes.

I will still use words like *blood* even when
I know they mean *ooze*. The only thrills
will be from what I can thieve:

retainer tucked inside a napkin,
a bracelet,
undelivered love letter.

Then one day
you will give me your wedding ring—
along with the rest of your pasta salad.

             And I know you will come back.

You will enter my house
which is really my body.
I will pretend the Jamba Juice lid curling

against your neck is my head,
that you know we are snuggling.
I will even believe

you are searching for me in here,
not the part of you
you have left.

You will say,
My God—
this is disgusting.

And for the first time
I will feel understood.

MIDNIGHT

Her: Are you there?
Me: I don't know how to answer that.

Her: Is it dark where you are?
Me: It's more the opposite of sight.

Her: Can you see?
Me: I've not learned the rules yet.

Her: You should see me.
Me: Does that mean you're alive?

Her: How much does that matter?
Me: I said your name aloud yesterday.

Her: I've kept yours in a box I made but never open.
Me: It sounded like words.

Her: What if I found you?
Me: No one understood I was speaking a different language.

Her: If you never hear me again, will you think I've forgotten you?
Me: I'll know when you've forgotten.

Her: What if it's never?
Me: I'm losing the letters from your name individually.

Her: Our names are holding us back.
Me: Your name is becoming a scent.

Her: Your name is becoming the box.

NOT ABOUT ME

My voice does not sing along with Billy Joel in the shower. It does
not paint the bathroom ceiling in the delicious murder of high
notes. I do not repeatedly *talk* myself along city sidewalks as if
words hold the ability to propel my body faster. I do not read
unbelievable pieces of literature, each line three or four times,
terrified everyone gets it but me. I do not then make reference
to how *the story captured me,* how it has *forever influenced my further
artistic movements.* I am not the white boy of your loose tongue—
the impersonal, all-encompassing, *white boy*—not me. I do not
sing, never. I am not human. I do not watch a blue-jeaned hip
twist to the beat of a stoplight on 17th Street, do not feel the
whistle and spit already bubble in my throat. I do not speak, but
when I do, I am not afraid my eyes have shown too much. I have
not wrapped myself completely around what you think of me.
I have never been persuaded to love without condoms. I never
called it *love* when it should have been called *penis,* called it *love*
when it should have been called *lonely,* called it *love* when it
should have been called *trying-too-hard.* My outer layer does not
mask my secrets well. I do not feel secrets pressing the walls
of my throat. I have never allowed ugly words to crawl inside my
cheeks, then splatter across walls. I will not sing. I will never be
a singer. I never named this voice, *Beautiful.* Never imagined the sky
was a goal we could accomplish. I never thought we were the sky.
People will always *people.* We do not name ourselves *Potential.* Our
skin is only a collection of cells. I do not name myself *Solution.*
Accountable is not a line in this story. Gravity will always keep us
stuck to this floor. These bones don't want out of this skin. I do
not wish to unlock my ribs, say, *Look—I made this.* I do not bleed.
I am giving you the entire story. You have already leafed through
my pages. You have seen the whole show. Your approval is not
my concern. I am not afraid to speak like there is something

at stake. I am not afraid to finish this poem. This poem is not about me. I do not want you to listen. I am not afraid. I am not afraid. I am not afraid. Afraid not I am. Afraid not am I. Not afraid I am. I do not bleed. I am not human. I am not here.

THANK YOU

Jeanann Verlee, Union Square to Sunnyside breakfast to the top of
a sky we have yet to visit. This is your lullaby. Your book. Adam
Falkner, my 360-degree magic maker, your grace is boundless,
there's not an itch in this world I won't scratch with you. Angel
Nafis, whatever God-sent meteor you had to lasso out there and
ride cowboy style (arms thrashing) to this rock, all I do is praise,
love, and continue dancing to each song it sings. Warner Asch and
Ben Ochstein, let this be a humble stopgap 'til we smoke cigars on
a porch and teach kids about the old days. Roger Bonair-Agard,
where you think I learned this shadowbox? This ode to sweat and
moon? Ben, I'll rip a leather jacket for you, zip around your wisdom
like an infinity sign—act like any of this is possible without you.
Jacob, I followed you south and don't think I ever came back. If life
is a metaphor for a dance contest, we're winning. Abe, you are my
hero and more. Every joke I got, I stole from you in this life or the
last. Chad, fuck a gene pool. Never been anything but a brother to
all things me. Eli, we are road maps that lead to you, we are in good
hands. Mom and Dad! Can you believe it? I'm you. Turns out I've
always been. All I do is love you. I'm doing it right now.

(Exhale)

Unending joy and appreciation to Ed Menchavez, Eboni Hogan,
Carlos Andres-Gomez, Rico Frederick, Geoff and Emily Kagan-
Trenchard, Lynne Procope, Ram Devineni, Mahogany L. Browne,
Mike McGee, Mindy Nettifee, Brian S. Ellis, and Sarah Kay,
who have always made these poems and this world better. Derrick
Brown and the entire Write Bloody family for allowing The Kid's
words such a beautiful bed to rest. Shira Erlichman, Ken Arkind,
and Danny Sherrard, whose friendship and support have meant
everything to these stories and the man who wrote them. Cristin
O'Keefe Aptowicz, for your astounding pool of wisdom and

direction. Rachel McKibbens, for the indispensable guidance of priorities. Lindsey, Mollie, and Wendell—very much my siblings. Michael Cirelli, Mikal, Parker, Jamilla, Marissa, the undeniable Reynold Martin, and the ridiculous crew of young people who make up the Urban Word family. The entire LouderARTS Project, past and present. Positive Health Project, Robert Childs, and the countless astounding individuals throughout New York City who have trusted me with their stories. Jeff Kearns (CJ) forever. JK Publishing, Designated Space, and the original Donkey Coffee Tuesday night crew in Athens, Ohio. To Art, Story, and Love—for having no off-switch. It has always been your star I wish to follow.

ABOUT THE AUTHOR

Jon Sands has been a professional teaching and performing artist since 2007. He is the Director of Poetry Education Programming at the Positive Health Project (a syringe exchange center in Midtown Manhattan), and delivered the 2010 commencement address at the Bronx Academy of Letters. In December of 2010 he toured throughout Germany in conjunction with the American Embassy, and played the lead role in the 2011 web-series "Verse: A Murder Mystery" from Rattapallax Films. He's a recipient of the 2009 New York City-LouderARTS fellowship grant, and has represented NYC multiple times at the National Poetry Slam. He lives in Brooklyn, where he makes better tuna salad than anyone you know.

ACKNOWLEDGMENTS

A heartfelt thank you to the following publications where previous versions of these poems first appeared:

Dance Macabre: "What I Know" and "My Friend"

decomP: "Empty" and "A Working List of Things I Will Never Tell You"

kill author: "White Boy," "Grab a Snack, Enjoy the Space, But If You're Not Supporting Us, Time to Split," and "The Day Time Left"

The Literary Bohemian: "The Fishermen" and "The Monster I'm Hiding Under My Bed Says"

Muzzle Magazine: "Not About Me" and "Passover (or Thursday)"

The November 3rd Club: "Highway 71"

Spindle Magazine: "I Got a Letter from Midtown"

Suss: "Party & Bullshit"

Got a Letter From Midtown (chapbook), JK Publishing: "Highway 71," "April 23rd," Turbulence," "Am," "I Got a Letter from Midtown," and "Not About Me"

NEW WRITE BLOODY BOOKS FOR 2011

DEAR FUTURE BOYFRIEND
A Write Bloody reissue of Cristin O'Keefe Aptowicz's first book of poetry

HOT TEEN SLUT
A Write Bloody reissue of Cristin O'Keefe Aptowicz's second book of poetry
about her time writing for porn

WORKING CLASS REPRESENT
A Write Bloody reissue of Cristin O'Keefe Aptowicz's third book of poetry

OH, TERRIBLE YOUTH
A Write Bloody reissue of Cristin O'Keefe Aptowicz's fourth book of poetry
about her terrible youth

38 BAR BLUES
A collection of poems by C.R .Avery

WORKIN' MIME TO FIVE
Humor by Derrick Brown

REASONS TO LEAVE THE SLAUGHTER
New poems by Ben Clark

YESTERDAY WON'T GOODBYE
New poems by Brian Ellis

WRITE ABOUT AN EMPTY BIRDCAGE
New poems by Elaina M. Ellis

THESE ARE THE BREAKS
New prose by Idris Goodwin

BRING DOWN THE CHANDELIERS
New poems by Tara Hardy

THE FEATHER ROOM
New poems by Anis Mojgani

LOVE IN A TIME OF ROBOT APOCALYPSE
New poems by David Perez

THE NEW CLEAN
New poems by Jon Sands

THE UNDISPUTED GREATEST WRITER OF ALL TIME
New poems by Beau Sia

SUNSET AT THE TEMPLE OF OLIVES
New poems by Paul Suntup

GENTLEMAN PRACTICE
New work by Buddy Wakefield

HOW TO SEDUCE A WHITE BOY IN TEN EASY STEPS
New poems by Laura Yes Yes

OTHER WRITE BLOODY BOOKS (2003 - 2010)

STEVE ABEE, GREAT BALLS OF FLOWERS (2009)
New poems by Steve Abee

EVERYTHING IS EVERYTHING (2010)
New poems by Cristin O'Keefe Aptowicz

CATACOMB CONFETTI (2010)
New poems by Josh Boyd

BORN IN THE YEAR OF THE BUTTERFLY KNIFE (2004)
Poetry collection (1994-2004) by Derrick Brown

I LOVE YOU IS BACK (2006)
Poetry compilation (2004-2006) by Derrick Brown

SCANDALABRA (2009)
New poetry compilation by Derrick Brown

DON'T SMELL THE FLOSS (2009)
New Short Fiction Pieces By Matty Byloos

THE BONES BELOW (2010)
New poems by Sierra DeMulder

THE CONSTANT VELOCITY OF TRAINS (2008)
New poems by Lea C. Deschenes

HEAVY LEAD BIRDSONG (2008)
New poems by Ryler Dustin

WRITE BLOODY ANTHOLOGIES

THE ELEPHANT ENGINE HIGH DIVE REVIVAL (2009)
Poetry by Buddy Wakefield, Derrick Brown,
Anis Mojgani, Shira Erlichman and many more!

THE GOOD THINGS ABOUT AMERICA (2009)
An illustrated, un-cynical look at our American Landscape. Various authors.
Edited by Kevin Staniec and Derrick Brown

JUNKYARD GHOST REVIVAL (2008)
Poetry by Andrea Gibson, Buddy Wakefield, Anis Mojgani,
Derrick Brown, Robbie Q, Sonya Renee and Cristin O'Keefe Aptowicz

THE LAST AMERICAN VALENTINE:
ILLUSTRATED POEMS TO SEDUCE AND DESTROY (2008)
24 authors, 12 illustrators team up for a collection of non-sappy love poetry.
Edited by Derrick Brown

LEARN THEN BURN (2010)
Anthology of poems for the classroom. Edited by Tim Stafford and Derrick Brown.

LEARN THEN BURN TEACHER'S MANUAL (2010)
Companion volume to the *Learn Then Burn* anthology. Includes lesson plans and worksheets for educators.
Edited by Tim Stafford and Molly Meacham.

WRITEBLOODY

WWW.WRITEBLOODY.COM

WRITEBLOODY
QUALITY AMERICAN BOOKS

PULL YOUR BOOKS UP BY THEIR BOOTSTRAPS

Write Bloody Publishing distributes and promotes great books of fiction, poetry and art every year. We are an independent press dedicated to quality literature and book design, with an office in Long Beach, CA.

Our employees are authors and artists so we call ourselves a family. Our design team comes from all over America: modern painters, photographers and rock album designers create book covers we're proud to be judged by.

We publish and promote 8-12 tour-savvy authors per year. We are grass-roots, D.I.Y., bootstrap believers. Pull up a good book and join the family. Support independent authors, artists and presses.

Visit us online:
WRITEBLOODY.COM